Salads

LYN RUTHERFORD

MEREHURST

LONDON

Contents

Managing Editor: Janet Illsley
Photographer: David Gill
Designer: Sue Storey
Food Stylist: Lyn Rutherford
Photographic Stylist: Maria Jacques
Typeset by Angel Graphics
Colour separation by J. Film Process Limited, Thailand
Printed in Italy by New Interlitho S.p.A.

Published 1990 by Merehurst Ltd,
Ferry House, 51/57 Lacy Rd, Putney, London SW15 1PR

© Merehurst Ltd

ISBN 1 85391 133 X

NOTES

All spoon measures are level: 1 tablespoon = 15ml spoon;
1 teaspoon = 5ml spoon.
Use fresh herbs and freshly ground black pepper unless
otherwise stated.

Introduction

Gone, thankfully, are the days when a salad meant a few limp lettuce leaves and a tomato quarter. Now an ever-increasing and exciting range of fresh fruit and vegetables is available throughout the year. Salad leaves come in a myriad of colours, in varying shapes and sizes, flavours and textures. Crisp and tender 'baby vegetables' are perfect for salads, too.

The only rule for delicious salads is that you must use the freshest possible ingredients. Choose bright, perky leaves and herbs, the crispest vegetables, and fruits in perfect condition. Wash all leaves, vegetables and fruit, then chop, slice or dice as you like. Unless a recipe states otherwise it is best to prepare salads as close to serving time as possible, to ensure they are at their brightest, crispest and most nutritious.

It is worth making a little effort to dress your salads well. Be adventurous – there are plenty of interesting vinegars and oils available. Buy good quality oils – such as virgin olive oil, grapeseed, walnut, hazelnut and sesame – expensive perhaps, but a little goes a long way. Use red and white wine vinegars, balsamic and herb vinegars, or try making your own flavoured vinegars – by adding herbs and garlic or spices to a basic wine vinegar.

I have included many of my favourite salad combinations in this book. I hope you enjoy them and feel inspired to create many more of your own.

Lyn Rutherford

Tomato, Cheese & Basil Salad

This ultimate tomato and mozzarella salad is a great favourite of mine. It looks superb arranged on a huge platter. Serve with a selection of breads as a starter, or with cold meats or fish as a colourful main course. To make a smaller quantity you can always omit the cherry tomatoes and chêvre.

500g (1lb) plum tomatoes
250g (8oz) cherry tomatoes, with
  tops left on
185g (6oz) mozzarella cheese,
  preferably made from buffalo
  milk
90g (3oz) chêvre, crumbled
3 tablespoons chopped sun-
  dried tomatoes
2 tablespoons chopped basil

DRESSING:
7 tablespoons virgin olive oil
3 tablespoons red wine vinegar
1 clove garlic, crushed
¼ teaspoon caster sugar
½ teaspoon Dijon mustard
salt and pepper to taste

1 Slice the plum tomatoes and arrange them overlapping on a large serving platter. Place the cherry tomatoes around the edge. Slice the mozzarella and arrange on top of the plum tomatoes. Sprinkle the salad with crumbled chêvre, chopped sun-dried tomatoes and basil. Cover with plastic wrap and chill until required.
2 To make the dressing, stir all the ingredients together in a small bowl or shake in a screw-top jar until combined. Just before serving pour over the salad. *Serves 4-6.*

NOTE: If plum tomatoes are unavailable use Provence tomatoes or any other large variety. Sun-dried tomatoes are available, usually preserved in olive oil, from Italian delicatessens.

Pear with Chicory & Cambozola

2 large ripe pears
2 small heads chicory (witlof),
   separated into leaves
250g (8oz) Cambozola, or other
   soft blue vein cheese
DRESSING:
2 tablespoons white wine
   vinegar

2 tablespoons walnut oil
½ teaspoon grated orange rind
pinch of sugar
salt and pepper to taste
TO GARNISH:
orange slices
parsley sprigs

1 First make the dressing: stir the ingredients together in a small bowl or shake in a screw-top jar until combined.
2 Peel, core and thinly slice the pears lengthwise. Arrange the pear and chicory (witlof) on individual serving plates. Pour over the dressing. Slice the cheese and arrange on the plates. Serve immediately, garnished with orange slices and parsley sprigs. *Serves 4.*

Melon & Parma Ham

1 small Chanterais melon
1 small Galia or Ogen melon
12 very thin slices Parma ham
DRESSING:
60g (2oz) dolcelatte
juice of ½ lemon

1-2 tablespoons olive oil
1 tablespoon cream or milk
pepper to taste
TO GARNISH:
mint sprigs

1 Cut the melons into thin wedges and arrange on individual serving plates with the Parma ham. Cover with plastic wrap and chill until required.
2 To prepare the dressing, using a fork mash the dolcelatte and lemon juice to a paste. Stir in the remaining ingredients.
3 Just before serving, spoon dressing over melon and garnish with mint. *Serves 4-6.*

Avocado, Mango & Chêvre Toasts

2 ripe avocados
1 large ripe mango
2 tablespoons olive oil
1 tablespoon lemon juice
1 tablespoon finely chopped
   parsley
pinch of sugar

salt and pepper to taste
CHÊVRE & WALNUT TOASTS:
185g (6oz) soft chêvre
2 tablespoons finely chopped
   walnuts
1 small, thin baguette

1 Halve, peel and stone the avocado and mango. Cut into slices and place in a bowl with the olive oil, lemon juice, parsley, sugar, salt and pepper. Toss gently to mix.
2 Mix together the chêvre and chopped walnuts. Cut the baguette into 12 even slices and lightly toast under a hot grill. Divide the cheese mixture between the toasts and grill until hot and bubbling. Serve immediately with the salad. *Serves 4.*

Eggs with Anchovy Mayonnaise

about 90g (3oz) lamb's lettuce
   (corn salad)
4 eggs, hard-boiled
2 teaspoons snipped chives

DRESSING:
5 canned anchovy fillets,
   drained
5 tablespoons mayonnaise
3-4 tablespoons milk
pepper to taste

1 First make the dressing: put the anchovies in a small bowl, mash with a fork and blend in the mayonnaise, adding enough milk to give a smooth, creamy consistency. Season with pepper.
2 Place the lamb's lettuce (corn salad) on individual serving plates. Halve the eggs and arrange on the plates. Spoon the anchovy mayonnaise over them and sprinkle with chives to serve. *Serves 4.*

Japanese-Style Dipping Salad

I love food that involves eating with the fingers. These two dips, served with a carefully prepared array of fresh crudités, make a wonderful 'help yourself' starter.

CRUDITÉS:
selection of vegetables suitable
   for crudités, such as mange
   tout (snow peas), halved baby
   corn cobs, carrot, radishes,
   spring onions (green shallots),
   canned waterchestnuts, etc.
CHILLI DIP:
4 tablespoons hot or sweet
   chilli sauce
1 tablespoon soy sauce
2 teaspoons sesame oil

½ clove garlic, crushed
2.5cm (1 inch) piece fresh root
   (green) ginger, crushed
PRAWN & HORSERADISH DIP:
185g (6oz) peeled prawns
3 tablespoons mayonnaise
2 teaspoons creamed
   horseradish
1 teaspoon lemon juice
salt and pepper to taste
TO GARNISH:
coriander sprigs

1 First prepare the crudités: blanch the mange tout (snow peas) in boiling water for 30 seconds, drain; blanch the corn cobs for 3 minutes, drain and halve. Using a potato peeler, pare the carrot into long thin 'ribbons'. Trim radishes and make 3 crosswise cuts through the top of each, taking care not to cut right through. Trim spring onions (shallots) and 'feather' the leafy ends with a knife. Place all the vegetables in a bowl of iced water until required; the carrot, radishes and spring onions (shallots) will curl and open out.

2 To prepare the chilli dip, mix together all the ingredients in a small bowl.

3 To prepare the prawn and horseradish dip, finely chop the prawns and mix together with the remaining ingredients in a small bowl. Alternatively place all the ingredients in a food processor or blender and process until almost smooth. Season with salt and pepper.

4 To serve, transfer the dips to serving dishes and arrange the crudités on a large platter to accompany. *Serves 4.*

Fried Scallops with Roquette

3 tablespoons olive oil
500g (1lb) scallops, halved if
   large
1 clove garlic, crushed
½ small red pepper, cut into
   matchsticks
1 tablespoon white wine vinegar

2 spring onions (green shallots),
   chopped
1 tablespoon chopped chervil
salt and pepper to taste
TO GARNISH:
chervil or parsley sprigs

1 Heat the oil in a frying pan. Add the scallops and cook, stirring, for 3-4 minutes until almost done. Add the garlic and red pepper and continue cooking for about 30 seconds. Over a high heat, stir in the vinegar, spring onion (shallot), chervil and seasoning.
2 Meanwhile arrange the roquette on individual serving plates. Top with the scallop mixture and cooking juices and serve immediately, garnished with chervil. *Serves 4.*

Warm Chicken Liver Salad

30g (1oz) butter
3 tablespoons olive or groundnut
   oil
500g (1lb) chicken livers, halved
1 tablespoon red wine vinegar
1 teaspoon wholegrain mustard
3 tablespoons brandy

salt and pepper to taste
about 250g (8oz) mixed salad
   leaves, such as frissé (endive),
   radicchio, red chicory (witlof),
   oakleaf lettuce
½ small red onion, thinly sliced

1 Heat the butter and oil in a frying pan. Add the chicken livers and fry over a high heat for 3-4 minutes, until sealed and browned on the outside but still pink and tender within. Add the vinegar, mustard, brandy and seasoning; toss gently.
2 Meanwhile line individual serving plates with the salad leaves and onion rings. Spoon chicken liver mixture on top and serve at once, accompanied by toast triangles. *Serves 4.*

Thai-style Prawn Salad

Oriental foods provide a splendid variety of colours and textures, as well as enticing flavours. In this Thai-style salad the flavour of the prawns is enhanced by the unusual prawn dressing. You can buy jars of prawn paste from specialist oriental food shops.

90g (3oz) mange tout (snow peas)
½ red pepper, cut into matchsticks
12 cooked king prawns, peeled
250g (8oz) can water chestnuts, drained and sliced
3 spring onions (green shallots), sliced
handful of coriander leaves, roughly torn

DRESSING:
juice of 2 limes
1 tablespoon prawn paste
1 tablespoon groundnut or safflower oil
½ clove garlic, crushed
2.5 cm (1 inch) piece fresh root (green) ginger, grated
pinch of caster sugar
salt and pepper to taste

1 First make the dressing: stir all the ingredients together in a small bowl or shake in a screw-top jar until combined. Set aside.

2 Top and tail the mange tout (snow peas). Blanch in boiling water, together with the red pepper, for about 30 seconds. Rinse and drain well. Transfer to a serving bowl and add the prawns, water chestnuts, spring onions (shallots) and coriander.

3 Pour the prepared dressing over the salad and toss lightly to mix. Serve immediately. *Serves 4.*

VARIATION: If you prefer use a variety of cooked seafood, such as squid, mussels, crab claws and scallops. This is a particularly good idea if you need a larger quantity of salad to serve more people.

King Prawns with Asparagus

A tangy lemony tarragon dressing enhances an already superb combination of asparagus, bacon and king prawns. Serve with crusty bread.

500g (1lb) asparagus
6 rashers streaky bacon, rinds
   removed
12 cooked Mediterranean (king)
   prawns, peeled
1/2 head red oakleaf or
   mignonette lettuce, torn into
   bite-sized pieces

about 60g (2oz) lamb's lettuce
   (corn salad) or roquette
DRESSING:
4 tablespoons olive oil
3 tablespoons tarragon vinegar
1 tablespoon lemon juice
2 tablespoons chopped tarragon
salt and pepper to taste

1 To make the dressing, stir all the ingredients together in a small bowl or shake in a screw-top jar until combined. Set aside.

2 Cook the asparagus in boiling salted water for 4-6 minutes, until just tender. Rinse under cold running water, drain and transfer to a bowl.

3 Preheat the grill to medium high. Cut the bacon rashers in half and wrap a half rasher around each prawn. Place on a foil-lined grill rack and grill for 3-4 minutes, turning once, until the bacon is crisp and the prawns are hot.

4 While the prawns are cooking, arrange the salad leaves on individual serving plates.

5 Add the cooked prawns and any cooking juices to the asparagus. Pour over the prepared dressing and toss lightly to mix. Arrange on top of the salad leaves and serve immediately. *Serves 4.*

VARIATION: When asparagus is not in season, or for a less expensive alternative, substitute 250g (8oz) mange tout (snow peas). Blanch for 1 minute only, then refresh as above.

Mussels in Garlic Vinaigrette

Be sure to accompany this salad with lots of warm crusty bread for mopping up the delicious tomato and garlic dressing.

1kg (2lb) mussels
1 shallot, finely chopped
90ml (3 fl oz/⅓ cup) white wine
or water
3 tomatoes, skinned
DRESSING:
6 tablespoons tomato juice

3 tablespoons virgin olive oil
2 tablespoons herb wine vinegar
¼ teaspoon caster sugar
1 clove garlic, crushed
salt and pepper to taste
TO GARNISH:
1 tablespoon chopped parsley

1 Scrub the mussels to clean thoroughly and remove the 'beards'. Place in a large pan with the shallot and the white wine or water. Cook over a high heat for 3-4 minutes or until the shells have opened. Drain, discarding the liquid along with any unopened mussels. Transfer the mussels and shallots to a serving bowl and leave to cool. Cut the tomatoes into wedges, discard the seeds and add to the mussels.

2 To make the dressing, stir all the ingredients together in a small bowl or shake in a screw-top jar until combined. Pour over the mussel salad, toss gently to mix and chill for at least 30 minutes.

3 Just before serving re-toss the salad and sprinkle with freshly chopped parsley to garnish. *Serves 4.*

Smoked Salmon Parcels

Smoked salmon bundles, tied up with chives and served with simply dressed salad leaves and toast triangles, make a pretty and elegant starter.

2 eggs, hard-boiled
125g (4oz) cream cheese
3 tablespoons double (thick)
  cream
2 teaspoons snipped chives
salt and pepper to taste
4 slices smoked salmon
few whole chives

about 125g (4oz) mixed salad
  leaves, such as chicory
  (witlof), red cos lettuce, frisée
  (endive), watercress, lamb's
  lettuce (corn salad)
DRESSING:
4 tablespoons olive oil
2 tablespoons lemon juice
¼ teaspoon Dijon mustard
pinch of sugar

1 Finely chop the hard-boiled eggs. Place in a bowl with the cream cheese, cream and chives and mix well. Season with salt and pepper.

2 Lay the smoked salmon slices flat and divide the cream cheese mixture between them. Roll or fold to enclose the filling. Tie each 'parcel', with whole chives to garnish and refrigerate, covered with plastic wrap, until required.

3 To make the dressing, stir all the ingredients in a small bowl or shake in a screw-top jar until combined. Season with salt and pepper to taste.

4 Just before serving put the salad leaves into a bowl, add the dressing and toss gently to mix. Arrange the salad leaves on individual serving plates with the salmon parcels. Serve with wholewheat toast. *Serves 4.*

Duck Breasts & Roquette Salad

Succulent breast of duck, with tangy orange slices, roquette and ribbons of courgette (zucchini), makes an elegant main course salad. You can cook the duck and prepare the dressing ahead, leaving little last minute preparation. Serve with new potatoes.

4 boneless duck breasts
2 teaspoons sesame oil
1 tablespoon olive oil
2 courgettes (zucchini)
2 oranges
about 60g (2oz) roquette
DRESSING:
4 tablespoons olive oil
1 tablespoon sesame oil

2 tablespoons red wine vinegar
2 teaspoons finely chopped
  parsley
1 teaspoon grated orange rind
pinch of sugar
salt and pepper to taste
TO GARNISH:
2 teaspoons toasted sesame seeds

1 Using a sharp knife make 3 or 4 diagonal slashes in the skin of each duck breast. Heat the oils in a large frying pan, add the duck breasts and cook over a fairly high heat for 5-7 minutes, turning once, until well browned on the outside and just pink within. Transfer to a plate and leave to cool.

2 To make the dressing, stir all the ingredients together in a small bowl or shake in a screw-top jar to combine.

3 Using a potato peeler, pare the courgettes (zucchini) into long thin 'ribbons'. Peel the oranges, removing all the pith, and slice thinly.

4 Arrange the courgettes (zucchini), orange slices and roquette on individual serving plates. Slice each duck breast and arrange in a fan shape on each plate. Spoon the dressing over the salads and serve immediately, sprinkled with toasted sesame seeds. *Serves 4.*

Hot Chicken Salad with Mango

Medallions of chicken, crisp mange tout (snow peas), cashews and ripe mango make a delicious combination – especially mingled with the flavours of sesame, lime and coriander. Be sure to use a mango that is ripe, golden and scented.

125g (4oz) mange tout
  (snow peas)
1 ripe mango
60g (2oz/¹/₃ cup) salted cashews
3 skinned chicken breast fillets
1¹/₂ tablespoons sesame oil
5 tablespoons groundnut oil
¹/₂ clove garlic, crushed

2 tablespoons sherry vinegar
grated rind and juice of ¹/₂ lime
pinch of sugar
pepper to taste
handful of coriander leaves
TO GARNISH:
1¹/₂ tablespoons toasted sesame
  seeds

1 Top and tail the mange tout (snow peas). Blanch in boiling water for a few seconds then refresh in cold water and drain. Peel the mango, cut flesh away from stone and slice thinly. Place in a salad bowl with the mange tout (snow peas) and cashews.

2 Cut the chicken breasts crosswise into thick slices and, using a rolling pin, flatten the slices between two sheets of greaseproof paper or plastic wrap to give thin 'medallions'.

3 Heat the sesame oil and 2 tablespoons groundnut oil in a large frying pan. Add the chicken pieces, a few at a time, and sauté for 2-3 minutes, turning once, until lightly browned and cooked right through. Transfer to a plate and keep warm until all the pieces are cooked.

4 Add the remaining oil to the pan with the garlic, sherry vinegar, lime juice and sugar. Season with pepper to taste and heat gently.

5 Add the chicken pieces to the salad with the lime rind and coriander leaves. Spoon over the dressing and toss gently to mix. Serve immediately, sprinkled with toasted sesame seeds. *Serves 4.*

Saffron & Mushroom Salad

Unusual mushroom varieties such as ceps, chanterelles, horn of plenty, morels and oyster mushrooms are often available from high class greengrocers and supermarkets. Whether you buy these mushrooms or pick them yourself, you will undoubtedly appreciate their superior flavours. Use a mixture of wild mushrooms or mix cultivated varieties such as chestnut, oyster and small cup mushrooms.

250g (8oz/1¼ cups) pearl barley
785ml (25 fl oz/3 cups) well-
flavoured chicken stock
¼ teaspoon saffron strands
375g (12 oz) wild mushrooms
4 tablespoons olive oil
1 shallot, finely chopped
250g (8 oz) cooked chicken,
diced

2 tablespoons white wine
vinegar
1 tablespoon finely chopped
parsley
salt and pepper to taste
TO GARNISH:
parsley sprigs

1 Put the pearl barley in a large saucepan with the stock and saffron. Bring to the boil, then cover and simmer for 20-25 minutes, until all the liquid is absorbed. Transfer to a large salad bowl and set aside to cool.
2 Meanwhile, slice or roughly chop any large mushrooms. Heat the oil in a large frying pan and sauté the mushrooms and shallot for 3-4 minutes, until tender. Using a slotted spoon, remove the mushrooms from the pan and add them to the barley with the chicken.
3 Add the vinegar to the cooking juices in the pan and cook over a high heat for about 1 minute to reduce by half. Pour over the salad. Stir in the chopped parsley and season with salt and pepper to taste. Allow to cool, cover with plastic wrap and chill for at least 30 minutes before serving.
4 To serve, toss the salad and garnish with sprigs of parsley. *Serves 4.*

Spiced Ham & Chicken Salad

An unusual but easily prepared salad of ham and smoked chicken, plums and salad leaves in a lightly spiced dressing. Do not confuse proper whole smoked chicken with the inferior compressed smoked chicken meat.

1 head radicchio, roughly torn
about 90g (3oz) lamb's lettuce
(corn salad)
185g (6oz) roast ham, cut into
julienne strips
250g (8oz) smoked chicken,
shredded
6 red plums, stoned and
quartered

DRESSING:
3 tablespoons groundnut oil
2 tablespoons red wine vinegar
1 tablespoon mango chutney
pinch of ground allspice
salt and pepper to taste
TO GARNISH:
2 tablespoons toasted pine nuts

1 Divide the radicchio and lamb's lettuce (corn salad) between individual serving dishes. Top each salad with roast ham, smoked chicken and plum quarters.

2 To make the dressing, stir all the ingredients in a small bowl or shake in a screw-top jar to combine. Just before serving, spoon the dressing over the salads and toss lightly. Sprinkle with toasted pine nuts to garnish. *Serves 4.*

Pork Stuffed with Prosciutto

Pork tenderloin is stuffed with proscuitto and sage, then roasted and sliced, to give pretty 'cartwheels' of delicious tender meat. Marsala wine cooking juices provide a good, rich dressing for this warm salad. Excellent served with new potatoes.

375g (12oz) pork tenderloin
90g (3oz) prosciutto, shredded
15g (1/2oz) sage leaves, shredded
4 tablespoons olive oil
155ml (5 fl oz/2/3 cup) Marsala
salt and pepper to taste

1/2 head lollo rosso or mignonette
    lettuce
about 185g (6oz) young spinach
    leaves
1 red onion, thinly sliced

1 Make a deep cut along the length of the pork tenderloin and open out to give a rectangle shape. Cut again along each half, taking care not to slice right through. Beat gently with a rolling pin to flatten the meat further and even out the shape.

2 Arrange the prosciutto and sage in a layer over the meat, roll up from the longest side and secure with string to give a long, neat sausage shape.

3 Preheat the oven to 220C (425F/Gas 7). Heat the oil in a large frying pan. Add the meat and cook over a high heat for 2 minutes, turning to brown and seal on all sides. Transfer the meat and juices to a small roasting dish. Pour over the Marsala and bake in the preheated oven for 15 minutes, turning the meat halfway through the cooking time.

4 Remove the meat from the roasting dish and strain the cooking juices into a small bowl. Season with salt and pepper to taste.

5 Arrange the lollo rosso or mignonette, spinach and onion on a serving platter or individual plates. Slice the stuffed pork fillet and arrange alongside the salad. Spoon the warm cooking juices over and serve immediately. *Serves 4.*

Deli Meat Platter

A large platter of delicatessen meats and salad garnishes makes a wonderful lunch or casual main course for guests to help themselves. Vary the cooked meats to include your favourites and be sure to supply plenty of warm crusty bread and butter.

1 x 470g (15oz) can artichoke hearts, drained
½ shallot, finely chopped
125g (4oz) selection thinly sliced salamis, such as Milano, Genoa, etc
60g (2oz) garlic sausage, sliced
60g (2oz) Bresàola (cured beef), sliced
60g (2oz) Coppa (cured ham), sliced
4-6 slices roast ham
2 large dill pickled cucumbers, thinly sliced

1 small bunch radishes
185g (6oz) cherry tomatoes
about 16 black olives
about 16 stuffed green olives
few lollo rosso or other salad leaves
MARINADE:
2 tablespoons olive oil
1 tablespoon white wine vinegar
1 teaspoon Dijon mustard
1 teaspoon chopped parsley
pinch of sugar
salt and pepper to taste

1 First make the marinade: stir all the ingredients together in a small bowl or shake in a small bowl or shake in a screw-top jar to combine.

2 Put the artichoke hearts and shallot in a bowl and pour over the marinade. Chill for at least 20 minutes before serving.

3 Arrange the cooked meats on a large serving platter with the salad ingredients. Drain the marinated artichoke hearts and add to the platter. Serve with grissini sticks, warm crusty bread and rolls. *Serves 4-6.*

Beef Niçoise

Rare cooked beef and new potatoes are particularly good flavoured with lots of wholegrain mustard. Here I have added French beans, tomatoes and olives for a superb and hearty Nicoise-style salad. Serve with French bread.

375g (12oz) beef fillet, cut into
    2.5cm (1 inch) thick steaks
freshly ground black pepper
500g (1lb) small new potatoes
125g (4oz) French beans, topped
    and tailed
16 green olives, preferably
    anchovy-stuffed
4 tomatoes, skinned and
    quartered
½ red onion, sliced

DRESSING:
5 tablespoons olive oil
2 tablespoons red wine vinegar
½ clove garlic, crushed
3 teaspoons wholegrain mustard
pinch of sugar
salt to taste
TO GARNISH:
chopped parsley

1 Preheat the grill to high. Season the beef liberally with pepper and grill for about 5 minutes, turning once, until well browned on the outside but still rare inside. Transfer to a plate and allow to cool.

2 Meanwhile, cook the potatoes in boiling salted water for 10-12 minutes until just tender. Allow to cool, then halve. Blanch the beans in boiling water, then refresh in cold water and drain. Transfer the cooked potatoes and beans to a large salad bowl and add the olives, tomatoes and onion. Slice the beef thinly across the grain and add to the salad.

3 To make the dressing, stir all the ingredients together in a small bowl or shake in a screw-top jar until combined. Pour over the salad and toss gently to mix. Sprinkle with chopped parsley to garnish. *Serves 4.*

Minted Lamb & Bulghur Salad

Strips of tender pink lamb and Mediterranean vegetables tossed with bulghur wheat in a minted citrus dressing. For a perfect summer meal accompany with tzatziki – the Greek yogurt and cucumber dip – lots of bread and chilled white wine.

250g (8oz/1⅓ cups) bulghur wheat
375g (12oz) boneless lamb steaks
4 tablespoons olive oil
1 small aubergine (eggplant), diced
90g (3oz) button mushrooms, halved
½ red pepper, finely diced
½ green pepper, finely diced
2 small courgettes (zucchini), thinly sliced

DRESSING:
4 tablespoons olive oil
2 tablespoons white wine vinegar
grated rind and juice of 1 lemon
1 clove garlic, crushed
2 tablespoons chopped mint
salt and pepper to taste
TO GARNISH:
mint sprigs

1 Put the bulghur wheat in a large bowl. Stir in 500ml (16 fl oz/2 cups) boiling water and leave to stand for 45 minutes, until all the liquid is absorbed.

2 Preheat the grill to high and grill the lamb steaks for 5-6 minutes, turning once, until well browned on the outside but still pink within. Transfer to a plate and allow to cool.

3 Heat the oil in a large frying pan, add the aubergine (eggplant) and mushrooms and sauté for 2-3 minutes, until just beginning to brown. Add to the bulghur with the peppers and courgettes (zucchini). Slice the lamb thinly across the grain and add to the salad.

4 To make the dressing, stir all the ingredients together in a small bowl or shake in a screw-top jar until combined. Pour the dressing over the salad and toss gently to mix. Serve garnished with mint sprigs. *Serves 4.*

VARIATION: For a seafood version, replace lamb with large prawns and mussels, and mint with dill or parsley.

Fruits de la Mer

A lavish special occasion seafood selection served with mayonnaise flavoured with lemon, tarragon and dill. Vary the seafoods as you like to include other fish goujons, lobster, oysters, etc.

90g (3oz/¹⁄₂ cup) dry white
  breadcrumbs
1 teaspoon garlic salt
1 teaspoon finely grated
  lemon rind
1 egg
375g (12oz) mixed fish fillets,
  such as lemon sole and
  salmon
oil for deep frying
155ml (5 fl oz/²⁄₃ cup) each dry
  white wine and water
375g (12oz) squid, cleaned
  and sliced

500g (1lb) mussels, scrubbed
6 cooked crab claws
12 cooked Mediterranean (king)
  prawns
DRESSING:
155ml (5 fl oz/²⁄₃ cup)
  mayonnaise
2 teaspoons finely grated
  lemon rind
1 tablespoon chopped dill
1 tablespoon chopped tarragon
TO GARNISH:
lemon slices
dill and tarragon sprigs

1 To prepare the fish goujons, mix together the bread-crumbs, garlic salt and grated lemon rind in a shallow bowl. Beat the egg lightly in a separate bowl. Cut the fish into strips and dip each first in egg, then in the breadcrumb mixture to coat evenly. Deep fry in batches in hot oil for 1-2 minutes until crisp, golden and cooked right through. Drain on absorbent kitchen paper and allow to cool.
2 Put the white wine and water in a saucepan and bring to the boil. Add the squid and cook for 2-3 minutes until tender then remove with a slotted spoon and leave to cool. Add the mussels to the pan and cook for 2-3 minutes until the shells have opened. Drain, discarding any unopened ones.
3 Arrange the prepared fish goujons, squid and mussels on a large serving platter together with the crab claws and prawns. Garnish with lemon slices, dill and tarragon.
4 To make the dressing, stir together the mayonnaise, lemon rind and chopped herbs in a small bowl. Serve with the seafood platter. *Serves 6.*

Smoked Haddock & Rice Salad

This salad is based on my own favourite kedgeree recipe and includes lots of whole spices for extra flavour.

185g (6oz) long-grain rice, cooked
3 eggs, hard-boiled and chopped
2 tomatoes, skinned and chopped
2 tablespoons snipped chives
500g (1lb) smoked haddock fillet
1 onion, chopped
1 bay leaf
1 tablespoon coriander seeds, lightly crushed

1 teaspoon cumin seeds, lightly crushed
315ml (10 fl oz/1¼ cups) milk
DRESSING:
1 clove garlic, crushed
3 tablespoons mayonnaise
pepper to taste
TO GARNISH:
lemon slices
few chives

1 Put the rice, chopped eggs, tomatoes and chives in a large salad bowl and set aside.

2 Put the smoked haddock, onion, bay leaf, crushed coriander and cumin seeds in a large frying pan, pour in the milk and bring to the boil. Immediately lower the heat until the liquid is barely simmering and cook for 8-10 minutes, until the fish flakes easily and is cooked through. Using a slotted spoon transfer the fish to a plate and allow to cool. Remove skin and flake the flesh. Add the fish to the salad.

3 To make the dressing, discard bay leaf from cooking liquid. Add the garlic and cook over a high heat for 1-2 minutes to reduce by half. Remove from the heat and add the mayonnaise, blending well until smooth. Allow to cool.

4 To serve, add the dressing to the salad and toss lightly to mix. Season with pepper and garnish with lemon slices and chives. *Serves 4.*

Assiette des Fromages

This is more of a cheese board than a salad but as a favourite lunch I feel it is worthy of inclusion here. You can vary the fresh salad ingredients as you like. Try for example radishes, carrot sticks, clementines, fennel, pear slices, apple, gherkins, cucumber etc.

1 demi-camembert
90g (3oz) Port Salut
155g (5oz) Roquefort
155g (5oz) mild goat's cheese
125g (4oz) strong goat's cheese
1 paw-paw (papaya)
2 sticks celery
1 small bunch grapes, about
  185g (6oz)

60g (2oz/²/₃ cup) walnut halves
4 fresh apricots
12 cherry tomatoes
about 60g (2oz) frisée (endive)
  or lamb's lettuce (corn salad)
TO ACCOMPANY:
warm French bread
savoury biscuits

1 Arrange the cheeses on a serving platter.
2 Peel and halve the paw-paw (papaya), discard the seeds and slice the flesh. Cut the celery into matchsticks. Arrange these on the platter with the grapes, walnuts, apricots, tomatoes and frisée (endive) or lamb's lettuce (corn salad).
3 Serve accompanied by warm French bread and a selection of savoury biscuits. *Serves 4.*

Vegetable & Nut Salad

250g (8oz) each carrots and
  courgettes (zucchini)
1 small fennel bulb, sliced
185g (6oz) cauliflower flowerets
60g (2oz) frisée (endive)
4 spring onions (green shallots),
  sliced
185g (6oz) Cheddar, diced
30g (1oz/¼ cup) walnut pieces

60g (2oz/⅓ cup) each salted
  peanuts and cashews, halved
1 tablespoon chopped parsley
1 tablespoon chopped chervil
DRESSING:
4 tablespoons mayonnaise
4 tablespoons natural yogurt
pepper to taste

1 Cut the carrots, courgettes (zucchini) and fennel into julienne strips and place in a salad bowl with the remaining ingredients. Toss gently to mix.
2 To make the dressing, stir ingredients together in a small bowl. Spoon over the salad just before serving. *Serves 4.*

Tomato & Roquefort Salad

1 head oakleaf or mignonette
  lettuce
6 tomatoes, roughly chopped
½ red onion, sliced
16 black olives
250g (8oz) Roquefort
1 tablespoon each snipped
  chives, chervil and dill

DRESSING:
3 tablespoons virgin olive oil
3 tablespoons walnut oil
3 tablespoons lemon juice
1 tablespoon red wine vinegar
½ clove garlic, crushed
pinch of sugar
salt and pepper to taste

1 Tear lettuce into bite-sized pieces and put in a salad bowl with tomatoes, onion and olives. Crumble in the Roquefort and add the herbs. Chill until required.
2 To make the dressing, mix ingredients together in a bowl or shake in a screw-top jar to combine. Pour over the salad and toss gently. *Serves 4.*

Gado Gado

This crunchy Indonesian salad with its spicy peanut sauce will appeal to vegetarians and non-vegetarians alike. Include other vegetables if you prefer, such as French beans, baby corn cobs or cauliflower.

2 tablespoons groundnut or
   olive oil
185g (6oz) firm tofu, diced
1 clove garlic, halved
185g (6oz) beansprouts
185g (6oz) leek
250g (8oz) carrot
250g (8oz) celery
125g (4oz) mange tout
   (snow peas), topped and tailed
185g (6oz) Chinese cabbage,
   shredded

PEANUT SAUCE:
30g (1oz) creamed coconut
4 tablespoons milk
½ small onion, chopped
1 clove garlic, crushed
4 tablespoons peanut butter
1 teaspoon soft brown sugar
2 teaspoons soy sauce
½ teaspoon ground cumin
½ teaspoon chilli powder
TO GARNISH:
1 egg, hard-boiled and finely
   chopped (optional)

1 First make the peanut sauce: chop the creamed coconut and place in a blender or food processor with the milk. Blend to a paste. Add the remaining sauce ingredients and puree until smooth.

2 Heat the oil in a frying pan, add the tofu and garlic and cook for 2-3 minutes, stirring gently, until the tofu is pale golden and beginning to crisp. Drain on absorbent kitchen paper and discard the garlic.

3 Arrange the beansprouts on a serving platter or in a shallow bowl.

4 Cut the leek, carrot and celery into julienne strips and blanch in boiling water for 1-2 minutes then refresh with cold water and drain thoroughly. Blanch the mange tout (snow peas) for 30 seconds; refresh and drain. Arrange the blanched vegetables, Chinese cabbage and tofu on top of the beansprouts.

5 To serve, spoon the peanut sauce over the salad. Sprinkle with chopped egg to garnish, if desired. *Serves 4.*

Broccoli, Bean & Almond Salad

The Szechwan peppercorns used in the dressing for this colourful salad impart a wonderful aromatic flavour. If they are unavailable, you can use freshly ground pepper to taste instead.

185g (6oz/1 cup) red kidney
beans, soaked overnight
90g (3oz/1/2 cup) mung beans,
soaked overnight
375g (12oz) broccoli flowerets
1 head radicchio
1/2 head oakleaf, lollo rosso or
mignonette lettuce
60g (2oz/1/3 cup) blanched
almonds, toasted
1/2 red onion, sliced

DRESSING:
5 tablespoons olive oil
3 tablespoons raspberry vinegar
pinch of soft brown sugar
1/2 teaspoon Szechwan
peppercorns, crushed
salt to taste

1 Drain the beans, place in separate pans and cover with fresh water. Bring to the boil and boil rapidly for 10 minutes. Lower the heat, cover and simmer until tender: allow a further 40-50 minutes for kidney beans; 10-12 minutes for mung beans. Drain and rinse under cold running water to cool, then drain thoroughly and place in a large salad bowl.

2 Partly cook the broccoli in boiling water for 2 minutes, then drain and refresh with cold water. Drain well and add to the beans. Tear the salad leaves into bite-size pieces and add to the salad with the almonds and onion.

3 To make the dressing, stir all the ingredients in a small bowl or shake in a screw-top jar to combine.

4 Just before serving pour the dressing over the salad and toss lightly to mix. *Serves 4.*

Wholewheat & Fruit Salad

Wholewheat – with its chewy texture and slightly nutty flavour – provides an excellent alternative to brown rice for vegetarian salads. I have chosen Wensleydale to complement the fruit but substitute your favourite cheese if you prefer.

185g (6oz/1 cup) wholewheat,
soaked
1 dessert apple
1 ripe pear
2 tablespoons lemon juice
90g (3oz) red seedless grapes
2 sticks celery, cut into
matchsticks
60g (2oz/½ cup) dried apricots,
chopped
60g (2oz/⅓ cup) pitted prunes,
chopped

185g (6oz) Wensleydale cheese
cubed
DRESSING:
5 tablespoons grapeseed oil
2 tablespoons white wine
vinegar
juice and grated rind of
½ orange
1 teaspoon chopped rosemary
salt and pepper to taste

1 Drain the wholewheat and cook in boiling water for 20 minutes until just tender. Rinse under cold water, drain thoroughly and leave to cool. Transfer to a large salad bowl.
2 Halve and core the apple and pear. Slice the apple and dice the pear, sprinkling with lemon juice to prevent discolouring. Add to the wholewheat with the grapes, celery, apricots and prunes. Stir in the cheese cubes.
3 To make the dressing, stir all the ingredients together in a small bowl or shake in a screw-top jar until combined. Pour over the salad and toss gently to mix. *Serves 4.*

Summer Chick Pea Salad

500g (1lb) cauliflower flowerets
1 x 440g (14oz) can chick peas,
drain
¹/₂ cucumber, thinly sliced
125g (4oz) alfalfa sprouts
handful of watercress sprigs
salt and pepper to taste

DRESSING:
90g (3oz) watercress
1 tablespoon chopped onion
125ml (4 fl oz/¹/₂ cup) thick sour
cream
2 tablespoons olive oil
1 tablespoon white wine vinegar

1 Cook the cauliflower flowerets in plenty of boiling salted water for 2 minutes. Rinse under cold running water to cool, drain well and transfer to a large salad bowl. Add the remaining ingredients and chill until required.
2 To make the dressing, purée the ingredients in a blender or food processor until smooth. Spoon over the salad just before serving. *Serves 4.*

Flageolet & French Bean Salad

250g (8oz) French beans
1 x 470g (15oz) can flageolet
beans, drained
about 60g (2oz) each frisée
(endive) and oakleaf lettuce
5 apricots, stoned and sliced
1 orange, peeled and sliced
30g (1oz/¹/₄ cup) walnut pieces

DRESSING:
5 tablespoons olive oil
3 tablespoons wine vinegar
1 teaspoon clear honey
1 teaspoon grated orange rind
salt and pepper to taste

1 Trim French beans and cook in boiling water for 3 minutes, then drain and refresh with cold water. Drain well and place in a serving bowl. Add remaining ingredients.
2 To make the dressing, mix ingredients together in a small bowl or shake in a screw-top jar to combine. Pour over the salad and toss lightly to mix. *Serves 4.*

Pasta Salad with Pesto

Pesto – the traditional Italian basil sauce – is adapted here to make a delicious dressing for a vegetarian pasta salad. Flavoured bread, such as walnut, onion or olive, makes a perfect accompaniment if you can obtain one. Otherwise serve any warm crusty bread.

500g (1lb) dried pasta quills
  (penne)
125g (4oz) French beans
125g (4oz) cherry tomatoes,
  halved
60g (2oz) button mushrooms,
  sliced
30g (1oz/¼ cup) pine nuts,
  toasted
few black olives (optional)

PESTO DRESSING:
8 tablespoons virgin olive oil
30g (1oz) basil leaves
30g (1oz) Parmesan, grated
4 teaspoons white wine vinegar
1 clove garlic, crushed
pepper to taste

1 Cook the pasta in plenty of boiling salted water for 7-8 minutes, until *al dente*, tender but firm to the bite. Rinse under cold running water to cool, drain well and transfer to a large salad bowl.

2 Top and tail the beans, then blanch in boiling water for 1 minute. Refresh in cold water and drain. Add to the pasta with the cherry tomatoes, mushrooms, pine nuts and olives, if using.

3 To make the dressing, place all the ingredients in a blender or food processor and purée for a few seconds until fairly smooth. Add to the salad and toss gently to mix. *Serves 4.*

VARIATION: Substitute other pasta shapes or wholewheat pasta as you like. For a more substantial vegetarian salad add 90g (3oz/¾ cup) cooked flageolet beans.

Brown Rice Salad

A substantial main course salad. For extra flavour, the rice is cooked as for a risotto – fried in a little butter, then simmered in stock. If available, use brown risotto rice for the best results.

30g (1oz) butter
½ small onion, chopped
315g (10oz/1½ cups) brown rice
125g (4oz) button mushrooms,
  quartered
750ml (24 fl oz/3 cups) hot
  vegetable stock or water
1 small green pepper, sliced
1 small red pepper, sliced
250g (8oz) frozen peas, thawed
3 eggs, hard-boiled
2 tablespoons chopped parsley
salt and pepper to taste

DRESSING:
6 tablespoons mayonnaise
4 tablespoons single (light)
  cream
1 teaspoon lemon juice
2 tablespoons snipped chives
TO GARNISH:
few chives
parsley sprigs

1 Heat the butter in a saucepan. Add the onion and fry gently for about 4 minutes until just beginning to brown. Stir in the rice and mushrooms and continue cooking, stirring constantly, for 2 minutes. Pour in the stock or water, bring to the boil, then cover and simmer gently for 20-25 minutes until all the liquid is absorbed.

2 Meanwhile to make the dressing, stir the ingredients together in a small bowl and set aside.

3 Stir the peppers and peas into the hot rice, transfer to a large bowl and leave to cool.

4 Chop 2 hard-boiled eggs and add to the salad with the parsley. Season with salt and pepper and toss gently to mix. Transfer to a serving dish and spoon over the dressing.

5 Slice the remaining hard-boiled egg and arrange on top of the salad. Garnish with chives and parsley. *Serves 4.*

Gourmet Vegetable Salad

Tender young vegetables are lightly cooked and tossed in a cooled hollandaise sauce to give a salad accompaniment worthy of any gourmet. This is a simple, no-fail hollandaise.

250g (8oz) new potatoes
½ cauliflower, cut into flowerets
185g (6oz) baby carrots
185g (6oz) courgettes (zucchini)
185g (6oz) sugar snap peas
185g (6oz) asparagus spears
HOLLANDAISE SAUCE:
3 egg yolks
1 teaspoon caster sugar

pinch of salt
juice of 1 lemon
2 tablespoons white
  wine vinegar
185g (6oz) butter
½ clove garlic, crushed
1 tablespoon chopped chervil
TO GARNISH:
chervil sprigs

1 First make the hollandaise: blend the egg yolks, sugar and salt in a food processor or blender for 2 seconds to mix. In a small pan, heat the lemon juice and vinegar and, with the machine on high speed, drizzle onto the egg yolks.

2 In the same pan, heat the butter with the garlic and chervil until bubbling. Drizzle onto the egg mixture at high speed as before, to give a smooth thick sauce. Transfer to a bowl, cover the surface with plastic wrap and allow to cool.

3 Meanwhile, cook potatoes in boiling salted water for 8-10 minutes until tender. Drain and cool; cut in half if large. Cook the cauliflower and carrots in boiling water for about 3 minutes until almost tender. Drain and cool.

4 Quarter the courgettes (zucchini) lengthwise and cut into 5cm (2 inch) lengths. Blanch, together with the sugar snap peas, in boiling water for 1 minute; rinse and drain.

5 Break off and discard the woody ends of the asparagus. Using a potato peeler, peel the stalks and cut in half. Cook in boiling water for 4-5 minutes until just tender; rinse and drain.

6 Put all vegetables in a large salad bowl. Spoon over the hollandaise and toss lightly. Garnish with chervil. *Serves 6-8.*

Asparagus in Tarragon Dressing

12-16 asparagus spears, about
  500g (1lb) total weight
DRESSING:
4 tablespoons olive oil
2 tablespoons tarragon wine
  vinegar
1 teaspoon grated orange rind

1/4 teaspoon Dijon mustard
1 tablespoon chopped tarragon
salt and pepper to taste
TO GARNISH:
orange slices
tarragon sprigs

1 Break off the woody ends of the asparagus spears. Using a potato peeler, thinly peel the stems. Cook in boiling water for 5-7 minutes until just tender, then refresh in cold water and drain. Transfer to individual shallow serving dishes.
2 To make the dressing, mix ingredients together in a small bowl or shake in a screw-top jar to combine. Pour over the asparagus spears. Chill for at least 30 minutes before serving.
3 Garnish with orange slices and tarragon sprigs. Serve as a delicious accompaniment to fish, chicken or egg dishes. *Serves 4.*

Classic Green Salad

2 'little gem' lettuce hearts
60g (2oz) frisée (endive)
1 head chicory (witlof), sliced
125g (4oz) mange tout (snow
  peas), blanched
3 spring onions (green shallots),
  sliced

1/2 cucumber, thinly sliced
DRESSING:
4 tablespoons olive oil
2 tablespoons wine vinegar
1 teaspoon clear honey
1/4 teaspoon Dijon mustard
salt and pepper to taste

1 Tear lettuce and frisée (endive) into bite-size pieces and place in a bowl with the remaining salad ingredients.
2 To make the dressing, mix ingredients in a small bowl or shake in a screw-top jar to combine. Add to the salad, toss lightly and serve immediately. *Serves 4-6.*

Summer Salad with Croûtons

A leafy salad with an abundance of summer herbs and edible flowers, plus crisp croûtons for extra crunch. For a special touch cut out shaped croûtons; toss them into the salad at the last minute to ensure they stay crisp.

250g (8oz) mixed salad leaves,
such as lamb's lettuce (corn
salad), escarole, radicchio,
frisée (endive), chicory
(witlof), four seasons lettuce,
watercress, nasturtium leaves
handful of herb sprigs, such as
chervil, dill, fennel
45g (1½ oz) edible flowers, such
as nasturtium, borage,
marigold

DRESSING:
3 tablespoons olive oil
2 tablespoons walnut oil
2 tablespoons wine vinegar
¼ teaspoon Dijon mustard
salt and pepper to taste
CROÛTONS:
3 thick slices white bread,
crusts removed
2-3 tablespoons olive oil
30g (1oz) butter

1 Place the salad leaves, herb sprigs and edible flowers in a large serving bowl.

2 To make the dressing, stir all the ingredients together in a small bowl or shake in a screw-top jar to combine. Set aside.

3 To make the croûtons, cut the bread into even-size cubes or cut into shapes using small pastry cutters. Heat the oil and butter in a frying pan until hot and sizzling. Add the bread and fry, stirring, for 3-4 minutes, until the croûtons are pale golden and crisp. Drain on absorbent kitchen paper and season with salt to taste.

4 Just before serving, pour the dressing over the salad and toss lightly. Sprinkle the croûtons on top. *Serves 4-6.*

Winter Green Salad

A crisp green salad tossed in a creamy dressing. Vary by including other winter vegetables, such as cauliflower, chicory (witlof) and green peppers, if you wish.

185g (6oz) hard white cabbage,
   shredded
1 small fennel bulb, thinly sliced
2 sticks celery, sliced
1 small leek, shredded
1 green apple, cored and sliced

DRESSING:
3 tablespoons mayonnaise
2 tablespoons natural yogurt
1/4 teaspoon celery seed
salt and pepper to taste
TO GARNISH:
celery leaves

1 Divide all the salad ingredients between individual serving bowls.
2 To make the dressing, mix the ingredients together in a small bowl. Add to the salad and toss lightly. Garnish with celery leaves. *Serves 4-6.*

Vegetable Julienne with Herbs

3 celery sticks
2 courgettes (zucchini)
2 carrots
1 small leek, about 125g (4oz)
DRESSING:
4 tablespoons olive oil
2 tablespoons white wine
   vinegar

6 teaspoons finely chopped
   mixed herbs, such as chives,
   parsley, chervil
1/2 teaspoon grated lemon rind
pinch of sugar
salt and pepper to taste
TO GARNISH:
chervil or parsley sprigs

1 To make the dressing, mix the ingredients together in a small bowl or shake in a screw-top jar to combine.
2 Cut the vegetables into thin matchsticks, or 'julienne' and divide between individual salad bowls. Pour the dressing over and toss gently to mix. Garnish with chervil or parsley. *Serves 4-6.*

Baby Corn & Almond Salad

500g (1lb) baby corn cobs
4 tablespoons groundnut oil
1/2 small onion, chopped
30g (1oz/1/4 cup) flaked almonds
2 tablespoons wine vinegar

1/4 teaspoon soft brown sugar
1/2 teaspoon grated lemon rind
salt and pepper to taste
TO GARNISH:
parsley sprigs

1 Unless they are very small, halve the corn cobs length-wise, Cook in boiling water for 3-4 minutes, until tender but still crisp. Drain and refresh under cold water, then drain well and place in individual serving bowls.
2 Heat 2 tablespoons oil in a small pan, add the onion and cook for 2-3 minutes, until softened. Transfer to a bowl.
3 Add the almonds to the pan and cook, stirring, for 1-2 minutes until lightly browned. Add to the onion with the remaining ingredients. Stir lightly, then spoon over the corn cobs. Garnish with parsley. *Serves 4-6.*

Fennel & Parmesan Salad

90g (3oz) piece Parmesan cheese
2 small fennel bulbs, thinly
  sliced
about 250g (8oz) young spinach
  leaves
1 red onion, thinly sliced
DRESSING:
4 tablespoons olive oil

2 tablespoons lemon juice
2 tablespoons double (thick)
  cream
1 tablespoon chopped fennel
  fronds
1 teaspoon grated lemon rind
1/4 teaspoon sugar
pepper to taste

1 Cut the Parmesan into wafer-thin slices and place in a bowl with the fennel. Toss lightly to mix.
2 Tear the spinach leaves roughly and arrange with the onion on individual serving plates. Pile the fennel and Parmesan mixture in the centre.
3 To make the dressing, stir all the ingredients in a small bowl. Spoon over the salad just before serving, as an accompaniment to grilled or barbecued meat and fish. *Serves 4-6.*

Sweet & Sour Vegetables

Crisp vegetables and fresh pineapple in a sweet and sour marinade make a tasty accompaniment to chicken, fish and pork dishes. This salad is especially good served as a side dish with oriental foods.

½ small cauliflower
1 carrot, sliced
½ pineapple
1 courgette (zucchini)
½ red pepper
½ green pepper
MARINADE:
5 tablespoons olive or groundnut oil

2 tablespoons sherry vinegar
2 teaspoons soy sauce
2 teaspoons tomato purée (paste)
½ clove garlic, crushed
¼ teaspoon soft light brown sugar
salt and pepper to taste
TO GARNISH:
1 teaspoon toasted sesame seeds

1 Break the cauliflower into small flowerets and partially cook, together with the carrots, in boiling water for 2 minutes. Refresh with cold water and allow to cool. Transfer to a bowl.

2 Peel the pineapple, remove the central core and roughly chop the flesh. Thinly slice the courgette (zucchini). Cut the peppers into thin strips and add to the salad with the pineapple and courgette (zucchini).

3 To make the marinade, stir all the ingredients together in a small bowl or shake in a screw-top jar to combine. Pour over the salad and chill for at least 1 hour before serving, sprinkled with toasted sesame seeds. *Serves 6.*

Garlic & Mustard Potatoes

625g (1¼lb) medium potatoes
4-5 tablespoons safflower oil
salt and pepper to taste
DRESSING:
4 tablespoons olive oil
2 tablespoons wine vinegar

1 clove garlic, crushed
1 tablespoon wholegrain
  mustard
TO GARNISH:
chopped tarragon or parsley

1 Partly cook the potatoes in boiling water for 5-6 minutes. Rinse under cold water until cool enough to handle, then slice thickly.
2 In a large frying pan, sauté the potatoes, in batches, in the safflower oil until golden brown. Drain on absorbent kitchen paper and transfer to a salad bowl. Season with salt and pepper to taste.
3 To make the dressing, stir all the ingredients together in a small bowl or shake in a screw-top jar to combine. Just before serving, spoon over the salad and garnish with chopped fresh tarragon or parsley. *Serves 4-6.*

Spiced Pineapple Salad

1 small ripe pineapple
½ teaspoon chilli powder
¼ teaspoon ground ginger
½ cucumber, sliced
1 red pepper, sliced
handful of coriander leaves

DRESSING:
3 tablespoons grapeseed or
  safflower oil
3 teaspoons lemon juice
pinch of sugar
salt and pepper to taste

1 Peel, core and chop the pineapple. Put into a bowl and sprinkle with the spices. Toss and let stand for 15 minutes.
2 Add the cucumber to the pineapple with the red pepper and coriander.
3 To make the dressing, mix the ingredients in a small bowl or shake in a screw-top jar. Just before serving, pour over the salad and toss lightly. *Serves 4-6.*

Onion Salad with Pecans

1 large Spanish onion
1 red onion
3 tablespoons thick sour cream
2 teaspoons chopped parsley
salt and pepper to taste

PECAN CHEESE BALLS:
185g (6oz) cream cheese
1 tablespoon snipped chives
¼ teaspoon paprika
16 pecan halves
TO GARNISH:
parsley sprigs

1 Thinly slice the onions and place in a bowl with the cream, parsley and seasoning. Toss lightly to mix.
2 To make the pecan cheese balls, in a bowl mix together the cream cheese, chives and paprika with seasoning to taste. Divide the mixture into 8 portions and shape into small balls. Sandwich each ball between 2 pecan halves.
3 Transfer the salad to individual serving plates and top with the pecan cheese balls. Chill for at least 30 minutes before serving, garnished with parsley. *Serves 4.*

Beetroot & Kabanos Salad

375g (12oz) new potatoes
250g (8oz) cooked beetroot, sliced
125g (4oz) Kabanos, Chorizo or other cooked spicy sausage, sliced
pepper to taste

DRESSING:
4 tablespoons thick sour cream
2 tablespoons mayonnaise
1 teaspoon German mustard
TO GARNISH:
dill sprigs
poppy seeds

1 Cook the potatoes in boiling water for 8-10 minutes until tender. Drain, cut in half and allow to cool. Transfer to a bowl and add the beetroot and sausage. Season with lots of pepper.
2 To make the dressing, stir the ingredients together in a small bowl. Spoon over the salad and toss well.
3 Garnish with dill and poppy seeds. *Serves 4-6.*

Aubergine & Mushroom Salad

This salad will keep in the refrigerator for a few days and makes a good accompaniment to cooked meats, or a delicious starter in its own right. Serve with crusty bread.

1 aubergine (eggplant), about
185g (6oz)
1 teaspoon salt
1 teaspoon coriander seeds
1/2 teaspoon cumin seeds
1/4 teaspoon fenugreek
5 peppercorns
6 tablespoons olive oil
2 cloves garlic, thinly sliced
1 shallot, finely chopped

1/2-1 red chilli, sliced
185ml (6 fl oz/3/4 cup) dry
white wine
375g (12oz) small whole button
mushrooms
2 tablespoons chopped coriander
leaves
TO GARNISH:
coriander sprigs

1 Dice the aubergine (eggplant) and put in a colander. Rinse with cold water, then sprinkle with salt and leave to stand for 25-30 minutes to degorge. Rinse again to remove the salt.

2 Lightly crush the coriander seeds, cumin and fenugreek with the peppercorns.

3 Heat the oil in a large pan, add the garlic and shallot and cook, without browning, for 5-7 minutes. Add the crushed spices, chilli and aubergine (eggplant) and cook for 3 minutes, until the aubergine is just beginning to soften.

4 Stir in the wine and mushrooms. Bring to the boil, then remove from the heat and stir in the chopped coriander. Allow to cool, then chill for at least 2 hours before serving, garnished with coriander sprigs. *Serves 4-6.*

Cucumber & Dill Salad

A delicate summery salad to accompany barbecued or grilled fish and chicken. If serving lamb, I use mint instead of dill.

1 cucumber
2 teaspoons salt
DRESSING:
3 tablespoons natural yogurt
1 tablespoon double (thick)
  cream

1 teaspoon chopped dill
pepper to taste
TO GARNISH:
lightly crushed cumin seeds
dill sprigs

1 Using a potato peeler remove most of the peel from the cucumber in strips, then slice very thinly. Put in a colander and sprinkle with salt. Leave to stand for 20-30 minutes, then rinse thoroughly. Drain and place in a serving dish.
2 To make the dressing, stir all the ingredients together in a small bowl.
3 Spoon the dressing over the cucumber and sprinkle with cumin seeds. Garnish with dill. *Serves 4-6.*

Date & Orange Salad

2 large oranges
375g (12oz) fresh dates, halved
  and stoned
1 head radicchio, roughly torn
60g (2oz) watercress sprigs
DRESSING:
1 shallot, finely chopped

4 tablespoons olive oil
2 tablespoons wine vinegar
1 tablespoon chopped parsley
2 teaspoons shredded orange
  rind
pinch of sugar
salt and pepper to taste

1 Peel the oranges using a sharp knife to remove all the pith. Thinly slice and arrange in a shallow serving bowl with the dates, radicchio and watercress.
2 To make the dressing, stir all the ingredients in a small bowl or shake in a screw-top jar to combine. Spoon over the salad and serve immediately, as an accompaniment to chicken, duck or beef. *Serves 4-6.*

Carrot, Celery & Caper Salad

375g (12oz) young baby carrots,
   halved lengthwise
3 celery sticks
2 tablespoons capers

DRESSING:
60g (2oz) blue cheese
2 tablespoons mayonnaise
4 tablespoons milk
pepper to taste

1 Partly cook the carrots in boiling water for 1-2 minutes so they remain crisp, then refresh in cold water and drain well.
2 Cut the celery into julienne strips and arrange on a serving plate with the carrots. Sprinkle with the capers.
3 To make the dressing, put the blue cheese in a small bowl and mash with a fork. Add the mayonnaise and milk and work until fairly smooth. Season with pepper. Spoon the dressing over the salad to serve. *Serves 4.*

Pasta & Olive Salad

250g (8oz) dried pasta twists
155g (5oz/1 cup) black olives,
   stoned
3 teaspoons olive oil
½ small onion, chopped
1 tablespoon chopped parsley

3-4 tablespoons double (thick)
   cream
2 teaspoons lemon juice
pepper to taste
TO GARNISH:
parsley sprigs

1 Cook the pasta in plenty of boiling salted water for about 7 minutes until *al dente*, tender but firm to the bite. Rinse and drain well, then put into a bowl. Slice 8 olives and add to the pasta. Allow to cool.
2 Heat the oil in a small frying pan. Add the onion and cook for 3 minutes until softened but not browned. Place in a food processor or blender with the rest of the olives. Purée for a few seconds to a coarse paste, then add the remaining ingredients and process briefly.
3 Add the olive paste to the pasta and toss well. Serve ganished with parsley. *Serves 4-6.*

Index